Hard and Soft

by Rod Theodorou and Carole Telford

Contents

Heinemann

First published in Great Britain by Heinemann Library
an imprint of Heinemann Publishers (Oxford) Ltd
Halley Court, Jordan Hill, Oxford OX2 8EJ

MADRID ATHENS PARIS FLORENCE PRAGUE WARSAW
PORTSMOUTH NH CHICAGO SAO PAULO SINGAPORE TOKYO
MELBOURNE AUCKLAND IBADAN GABORONE JOHANNESBURG

Illustrations by Sheila Townsend and Trevor Dunton
Colour reproduction by Track QSP
Printed in China

99 98 97 96
10 9 8 7 6 5 4 3 2 1

ISBN 0 431 06396 6

British Library Cataloguing in Publication Data
Telford, Carole
  Hard and Soft. – (Animal Opposites Series)
  I. Title II. Theodorou, Rod III. Series
  591

Photographic acknowledgements
Breck P Kent/Animals Animals/OSF p4; P Morris/Ardea London Ltd p5; Kjell B Sandvec/OSF p6;
Kevin and Cat Sweeney/Tony Stone Images p7; Paul Kay/OSF pp8 *top*, 14, 19, back cover; E.R Degginger/OSF p8
bottom; Zig Leszczynski/OSF p9 *left*; Howard Hall/OSF p9 *right*, back cover; David Curl/OSF p10 *left*; G.I Bernard/
OSF pp10 *centre*, 12, 16, 20 *right*; David Thompson/OSF p10 *right*; Fred Bavendam/OSF pp11, 21 *left*; Andrew G.
Wood Photo Researchers/OSF p13; Norbert Wu/OSF p15 *left*; Rudie Kuiter/OSF pp15 *right*, 21 *right*; Daryl Torkler/
Tony Stone Images p17; Tui De Roy/OSF p18 *left*; Colin Milkins/OSF p18 *right*; John Cooke/OSF p20 *left*
Front cover: Kjell B Sandvec/OSF *left*; Kevin and Cat Sweeny/TSW *right*

crab

armadillo

scorpion

Some animals are hard.
Some animals are soft.

slug

octopus

jellyfish

3

This is a crab.
A crab has a hard shell.

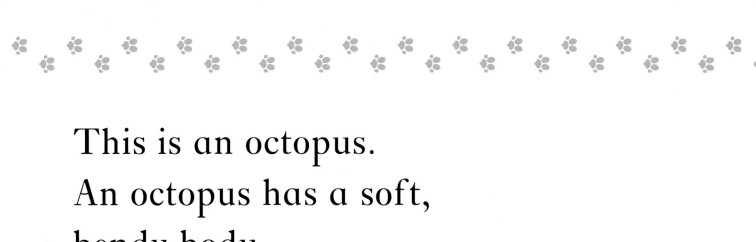

This is an octopus.
An octopus has a soft,
bendy body.

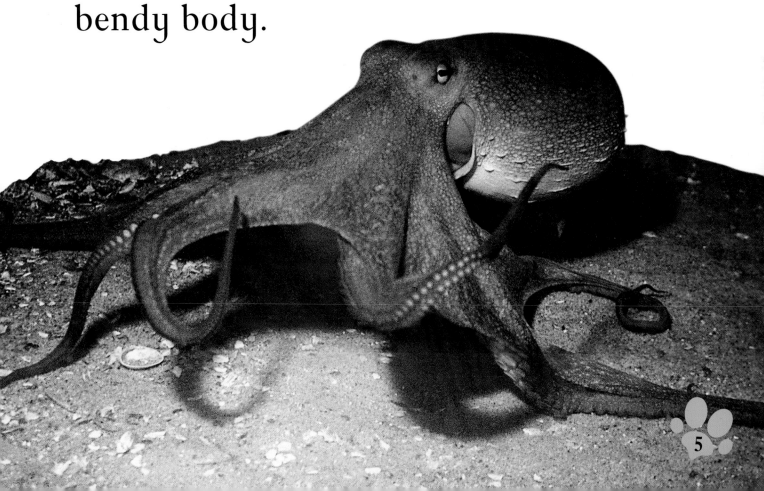

Crabs have ten legs.
The two front legs have
big claws.

Octopuses have eight legs
called tentacles.
Each tentacle has round suckers
for catching crabs.

tentacle suckers

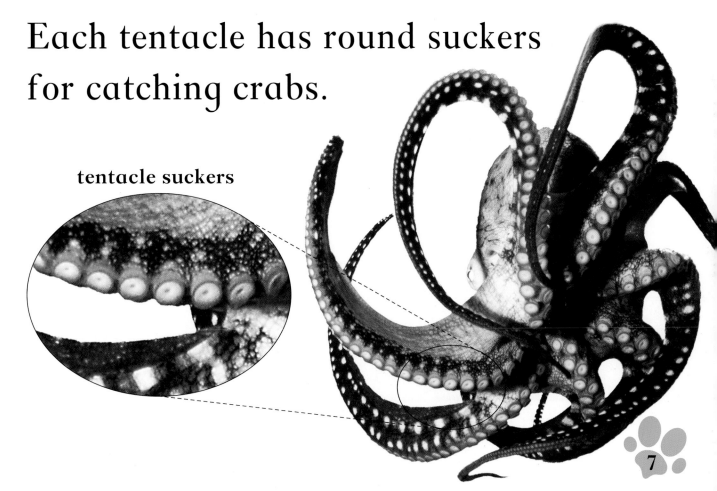

Most crabs
walk along
the bottom of
the sea.

Some crabs
live on land.

Octopuses also
crawl along
the bottom of
the sea.
They can swim too.

9

Crabs live under rocks.
Some land crabs dig burrows.

Most octopuses make their homes in caves. This octopus is curled up in a broken bottle!

Crabs have feelers covered in tiny hairs.
The feelers can smell food nearby.

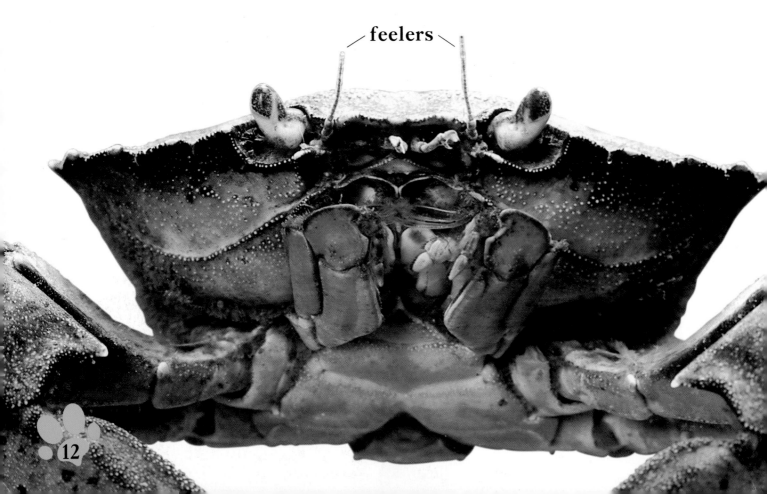

feelers

Octopuses have good eyesight.
They can see well in the dark.

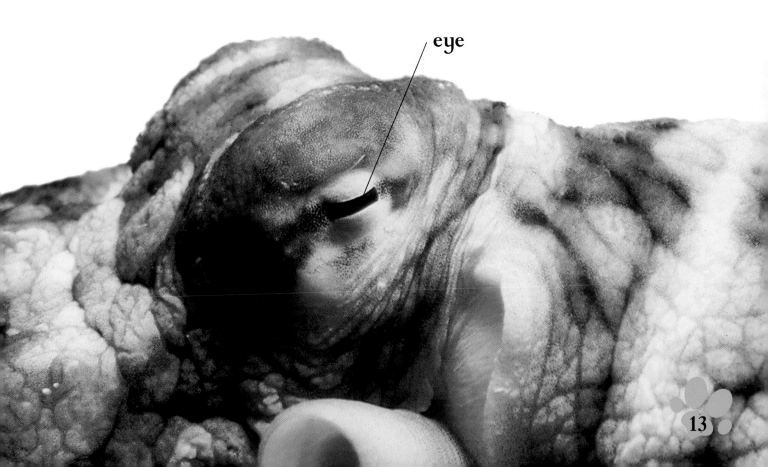

eye

A crab's hard shell and
claws protect it from enemies.

An octopus has a special trick to hide from its enemies.
It can change colour!

Some crabs bury themselves to
hide from enemies.

ink

Octopuses can bury themselves
in the sand too.
They can also squirt ink at an
enemy.

Crabs catch and eat fish with their strong claws.
They even eat other crabs.

hermit crab

Octopuses love to eat crabs.
They wrap their tentacles around
crabs and bite them.

crab going into the mouth

Crabs lay eggs.
Some crabs carry their eggs until
the eggs hatch.

baby crab

eggs

Octopuses lay eggs too.
Some lay their eggs in caves.

eggs

baby octopus hatching

AMAZING FACTS!

Some octopuses have a poisonous bite.

The blue ringed octopus is one of the most poisonous animals in the world!

The Pacific octopus has
tentacles 2 metres long!

Giant spider crabs can grow as
long as a car!

Index